INSIDE THE NFL

Seattle Seahawks

BY
RAMEY TEMPLE

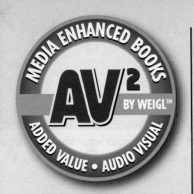

AV² provides enriched content that supplements and complements this book. Weigl's AV² books strive to create inspired learning and engage young minds in a total learning experience.

Your AV² Media Enhanced books come alive with...

Audio
Listen to sections of the book read aloud.

Key Words
Study vocabulary, and complete a matching word activity.

Go to **www.av2books.com**, and enter this book's unique code.

Video
Watch informative video clips.

Quizzes
Test your knowledge.

BOOK CODE

S 3 6 0 6 1

Embedded Weblinks
Gain additional information for research.

Slide Show
View images and captions, and prepare a presentation.

AV² by Weigl brings you media enhanced books that support active learning.

Try This!
Complete activities and hands-on experiments.

... and much, much more!

Published by AV² by Weigl
350 5ᵗʰ Avenue, 59ᵗʰ Floor
New York, NY 10118
Websites: www.av2books.com   www.weigl.com

Library of Congress Control Number: 2014930780

ISBN 978-1-4896-0890-1 (hardcover)
ISBN 978-1-4896-0892-5 (single-user eBook)
ISBN 978-1-4896-0893-2 (multi-user eBook)

Printed in the United States of America in North Mankato, Minnesota
1 2 3 4 5 6 7 8 9 0 18 17 16 15 14

042014
WEP150314

Project Coordinator Aaron Carr
Art Director Terry Paulhus

Photo Credits
Every reasonable effort has been made to trace ownership and to obtain permission to reprint copyright material. The publishers would be pleased to have any errors or omissions brought to their attention so that they may be corrected in subsequent printings.

Weigl acknowledges Getty Images as its primary image supplier for this title.

Seattle Seahawks

CONTENTS

Introduction

Despite starting off slowly over their first five seasons from 1976 to 1981, the Seattle Seahawks were fully supported by their fans. These fans would later be called the 12th Man. They went on to set world records for stadium noise. This is why the Seahawks are believed to have the greatest home field advantage in sports.

When coach Chuck Knox was hired in 1983, the Hawks began to win routinely for the first time, falling just a game short of the **Super Bowl**. The franchise continued moving closer to its main goal in 2005 under coach Mike Holmgren. They made their first trip to the Super Bowl, thanks in part to **most valuable player (MVP)** Shaun Alexander.

In the 2012 and 2013 regular seasons, the Seahawks only lost one home game while putting together a 15-1 win-loss record at CenturyLink Field.

On February 2, 2014, with coach Pete Carroll and the 12t^h Man leading the way, the Seahawks played in Super Bowl XLVIII. Russell Wilson, Marshawn Lynch, and one of the greatest defenses of all time helped the Seahawks crush the Denver Broncos, 43-8.

Russell Wilson has been the starting quarterback for the Seahawks since 2012.

SEATTLE SEAHAWKS

Stadium	CenturyLink Field
Division	National Football Conference (NFC) West
Head coach	Pete Carroll
Location	Seattle, Washington
Super Bowl titles	2013
Nicknames	The Hawks

12
Playoff Wins

1
Super Bowl Championship

8
Division Titles

History

HAWKS IN HISTORY

CORTEZ KENNEDY

was the most recent Seahawk to have his jersey retired. In 2012, Kennedy joined the 12th Man, Walter Jones, and Steve Largent in this exclusive club.

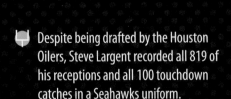

Despite being drafted by the Houston Oilers, Steve Largent recorded all 819 of his receptions and all 100 touchdown catches in a Seahawks uniform.

n 1976, the Seahawks and the Tampa Bay Buccaneers were the first two **expansion teams** created after the American Football League (AFL)-National Football League (NFL) **merger**. Aside from a near run to the Super Bowl behind Curt Warner and his 1,449 rushing yards in 1983, the Seahawks did not do much winning during the early years. The Pacific Northwest fans provided the Hawks with a great home field advantage anyway, living up to the nickname the 12th Man.

All-time great Steve Largent helped the Hawks capture their first division title in 1988, but retired the following season. By 1992, the Seahawks had bottomed out, finishing 2-14. Things started to change when Mike Holmgren took over in 1999, as he brought the Hawks back to the **playoffs** for the first time in 11 years. By 2004, the Seahawks had changed into the bullies of the NFC West, winning six division titles over the next 10 seasons.

The hiring of John Schneider and Pete Carroll in 2010 led to a flurry of smart draft picks, **free agent** signings, and trades. These roster moves helped build the framework for one of the greatest defenses in National Football League (NFL) history. By 2013, with rising star Russell Wilson behind center, the Seahawks earned their first Super Bowl championship.

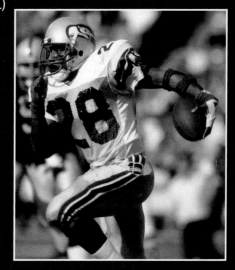

Curt Warner rushed for 6,705 of his 6,844 career rushing yards as a Seahawks running back.

The Stadium

CenturyLink Field holds 67,000 screaming Seahawks fans.

The Seahawks began to play in 1976 at the Kingdome, an indoor stadium in the South of Downtown neighborhood of Seattle. When it first opened, the Kingdome was home to the Seahawks, Mariners, and the SuperSonics. After the 1999 season, the Seahawks became the final pro team to leave the Kingdome, temporarily moving to Husky Stadium while their state-of-the-art facility was being built. On March 26, 2000, with crowds of people gathered to watch, the Kingdome was demolished.

The Seahawks fans are among the loudest in the NFL. Together, they are known as the 12th Man.

Seahawks owner Paul Allen was closely involved with the design of CenturyLink Field, stressing the importance of a small, open air stadium. The result of his vision was a modern stadium with views of the Seattle skyline. First known as Seahawks Stadium, the name was changed to Qwest Field two years after opening. When CenturyLink purchased Qwest in 2011, the stadium changed names again. Although there are NFL stadiums that seat more fans, there is no stadium quite as loud as CenturyLink. In fact, in 2013, the 12th Man broke the Guinness World Record for loudest crowd noise at an outdoor stadium.

 Along with more classic game food like pizza and hotdogs, Seahawks fans can chow down on cupcakes.

Where They Play

CANADA

Washington **30**

Oregon

Montana

North Dakota

Minnesota

Lake Superior

23 Wisconsin

22

Idaho

South Dakota

Iowa

24

29

Nevada

Utah

Wyoming

Nebraska

14

13 Illinois

15

California

Colorado

Kansas

Missouri

31

UNITED STATES

16

Arizona

New Mexico

Oklahoma

Arkansas

32

Texas

17

Mississippi

Pacific Ocean

Louisiana

12

27

Alaska

Hawai'i

MEXICO

Gulf of Mexico

0   500 Miles
0   500 km

0   100 Miles
0   100 km

AMERICAN FOOTBALL CONFERENCE

EAST	NORTH	SOUTH	WEST
1 Gillette Stadium	5 FirstEnergy Stadium	9 EverBank Field	13 Arrowhead Stadium
2 MetLife Stadium	6 Heinz Field	10 LP Field	14 Sports Authority Field at Mile High
3 Ralph Wilson Stadium	7 M&T Bank Stadium	11 Lucas Oil Stadium	15 O.co Coliseum
4 Sun Life Stadium	8 Paul Brown Stadium	12 NRG Stadium	16 Qualcomm Stadium

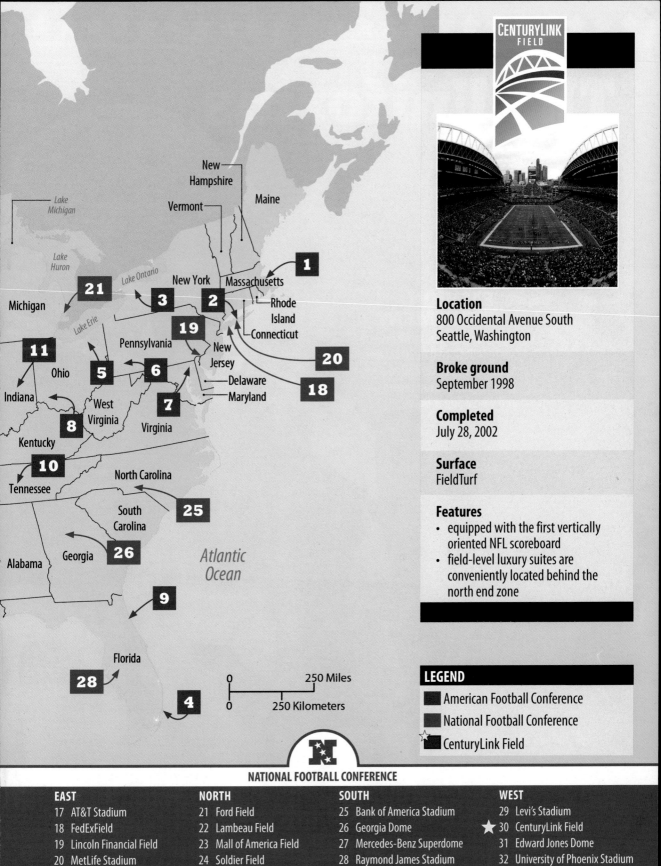

CENTURYLINK FIELD

Location
800 Occidental Avenue South
Seattle, Washington

Broke ground
September 1998

Completed
July 28, 2002

Surface
FieldTurf

Features
- equipped with the first vertically oriented NFL scoreboard
- field-level luxury suites are conveniently located behind the north end zone

LEGEND
- American Football Conference
- National Football Conference
- ⭐ CenturyLink Field

New Hampshire
Maine
Vermont
Massachusetts
Lake Michigan
Lake Huron
Lake Ontario
Michigan
New York
Rhode Island
Connecticut
Lake Erie
Pennsylvania
New Jersey
Ohio
Delaware
Indiana
West Virginia
Maryland
Kentucky
Virginia
Tennessee
North Carolina
South Carolina
Alabama
Georgia
Atlantic Ocean
Florida

1
21
3
2
19
20
18
11
5
6
7
8
10
25
26
9
28
4

0 ————— 250 Miles
0 ————— 250 Kilometers

NATIONAL FOOTBALL CONFERENCE

EAST	NORTH	SOUTH	WEST
17 AT&T Stadium	21 Ford Field	25 Bank of America Stadium	29 Levi's Stadium
18 FedExField	22 Lambeau Field	26 Georgia Dome	⭐ 30 CenturyLink Field
19 Lincoln Financial Field	23 Mall of America Field	27 Mercedes-Benz Superdome	31 Edward Jones Dome
20 MetLife Stadium	24 Soldier Field	28 Raymond James Stadium	32 University of Phoenix Stadium

The Uniforms

FASHION STATEMENT

After the team's uniforms were redesigned in 2002, the Seahawks have compiled a 24-8 regular season record and won a Super Bowl.

Richard Sherman's 20 interceptions from 2011 to 2013 led the NFL.

HOME

The Seahawks **logo** debuted in 1976 as a blue and green osprey, which is a large bird of prey. The design was inspired by Northwestern tribal art. Uniforms were blue and white, with blue and green arm stripes, accented by silver helmets and pants.

AWAY

By 2002, the logo and uniforms went through a complete redesign. The colors were changed to a lighter blue, contrasted with a darker blue, all highlighted by a lime green piping. The logo was changed as well in 2002, giving the osprey an arched eyebrow and focused eye, suggesting aggressiveness. In 2012, Nike became the official uniform supplier for the NFL, and updated the Seahawks' uniform and logo with feather-like trim and bolder colors.

The main three colors that make up the redesigned Seahawks uniforms are Wolf Grey, College Navy, and Action Green.

The Helmets

ONE AND ONLY

Despite having three different jersey colors and three unique pants options, the Seahawks only have one helmet.

A chinstrap keeps the helmet in place. All players are required to buckle their chinstraps before a play begins.

SPEED

The original 1976 Seahawks helmet was gray with the Seahawks logo decorating the sides in royal blue and forest green. This was accented by a gray facemask, which turned blue seven years later in 1983.

The helmets remained basically unchanged until 2002, when the Seahawks moved into the NFC West and their new stadium. Not only did the helmets go from gray to blue, but the logo was updated to suggest an angrier osprey.

In 2012, Nike changed the helmets to work alongside the new uniforms it designed. The new color scheme was built to mirror the colors of the Pacific Northwest wilderness. The new helmet included a 12-feather-pattern graphic, which represents the Seahawks faithful 12th Man. The logo on the helmet was also made both bigger and bolder, connecting at a point near the back of the player's head.

Despite the fact that Riddell was the NFL's official helmet manufacturer until October 2013, players can wear any helmet that meets the basic safety requirements.

The Coaches

7 Seven head coaches tried to bring a Super Bowl title to the Pacific Northwest before Pete Carroll finally succeeded.

By coaching University of Southern California (USC) to a college football national title, and Seattle to a Super Bowl victory, Pete Caroll became just the third coach to achieve both.

The Seahawks have been largely influenced by the leadership of three men. Chuck Knox was responsible for many firsts during his nine seasons as coach, beginning in 1983. Mike Holmgren took over in 1999 and won five division titles and a Super Bowl berth. A decade later, Pete Carroll rebuilt a roster around speed and youth, claiming the first championship in team history.

CHUCK KNOX

During his first year as head coach in 1983, Knox led the Hawks to a playoff berth. They went on to beat the Broncos and Miami Dolphins. With a trip to the Super Bowl at stake, they fell short to the Oakland Raiders. Knox went on to coach the Hawks for eight more mostly winning seasons.

MIKE HOLMGREN

In his first season with the club in 1999, Holmgren led the Seahawks to the **postseason** for the first time in more than a decade. During his next nine years, the Hawks won four straight NFC West division titles, an NFC Championship, and earned their first-ever trip to the Super Bowl.

PETE CARROLL

In his first season in 2010, Carroll almost completely changed the Seahawks roster. Two years later, he took a chance by starting a rookie quarterback named Russell Wilson. These moves paved the way for the Hawks' rise to the top of the NFL, capturing their first Super Bowl championship in 2014.

The Mascot

Blitz was born in the Kingdome, but now lives at CenturyLink Field.

Since 1998, the official mascot of the Seahawks has been Blitz, a large blue plush bird sporting bodybuilder muscles and a Seahawks number zero jersey. Blitz has changed his appearance slightly over the years, most notably to match the new uniforms and color schemes. In 2004, Blitz was given friendlier facial features, as he was scaring children while walking the sidelines at home games, and at community and charity events around Seattle.

 Taima the Hawk stayed uncaged in a hotel room in New York City leading up to Super Bowl XXVIII.

Since a Seahawk is an imaginary animal, the fans chose an augur hawk as their unofficial mascot. They voted to name him Taima, which means "thunder." This real life Hawk has led the Seahawks out of the tunnel at CenturyLink Field since 2007.

Blitz's hobbies include reading, fitness, and bird watching.

Legends of the Past

Many great players have suited up in the Seahawks' navy and green. A few of them have become icons of the team and the city it represents.

Cortez Kennedy

The Seahawks selected Cortez Kennedy with the third overall pick in the 1990 draft, and he blossomed into a defense star right away. In 1991, Kennedy was named to the Pro Bowl in just his second season in the league. In his third season, he was named NFL Defensive Player of the Year behind 14 **sacks**. When Kennedy retired after the 2000 season, he had recorded 668 tackles and 58 sacks in just 167 games with Seattle. He was elected to the Hall of Fame in 2012.

Position Defensive Tackle
Seasons 11 (1990–2000)
Born August 23, 1968, in Osceola, Arkansas

Steve Largent

Position Wide Receiver
Seasons 13 (1976–1989)
Born September 28, 1954, in Tulsa, Oklahoma

In 13 seasons as a Seahawk, Largent made it to the **Pro Bowl** seven times. Although he was not a speedy receiver, he was incredibly sure-handed. Largent retired holding almost every NFL receiving record, including receptions (819), receiving yards (13,089), and touchdowns (100). He also set a record by catching a pass in 177 straight regular-season games. The Pro Football **Hall of Fame** inducted him in 1995, and in 1999, Largent was honored as number 46 on the Sporting News' list of the 100 Greatest Football Players.

Shaun Alexander

In just his second season with the Hawks, Alexander loudly announced his presence by rushing for a franchise record 266 yards in a game against the Raiders. Four years later in 2005, Alexander went on to set the NFL single season touchdown record at 28. During that same magical season, he joined Emmitt Smith, Priest Holmes, and Marshall Faulk as the only running backs to record back-to-back 20 touchdown seasons. Also in 2005, Alexander captured his first NFL rushing title while leading the Hawks to the Super Bowl.

Position Running Back
Seasons 9 (2000–2008)
Born August 30, 1977, in Florence, Kentucky

Walter Jones

During 13 seasons with the Seahawks, Jones went to nine Pro Bowls and was an **All-Pro** selection seven times. Jones paved the way for Shaun Alexander during the 2005 season, helping the Seahawks reach Super Bowl XL. Despite 5,500 passes being attempted with Jones on the field, he gave up just 23 quarterback sacks and was called for holding just nine times. Coach Holmgren referred to Jones as the best offensive player he had ever coached. Jones is widely considered one of the greatest offensive linemen in NFL history.

Position Offensive Tackle
Seasons 12 (1997–2009)
Born January 19, 1974, in Aliceville, Alabama

Stars of Today

Today's Seahawks team is made up of many young, talented players who have proven that they are among the best players in the league.

Russell Wilson

Seahawks fans were shocked when coach Carroll named Wilson, a rookie third round draft pick, his starting quarterback in 2012. In his rookie season, Wilson made Carroll look like a genius, winning 11 regular season games and earning a playoff victory over the New Orleans Saints. Wilson finished fourth in the NFL in **passer rating** that season, breaking the previous rookie record. In tossing 26 touchdown passes, Wilson also tied the rookie touchdown pass record. His mobile and exciting style of play has earned him comparisons to hall of fame great Fran Tarkenton. In his second year in the league, Wilson led the Seahawks to their first Super Bowl championship.

Position Quarterback
Seasons 2 (2012–2013)
Born November 29, 1988, in Cincinnati, Ohio

Marshawn Lynch

Position Running Back
Seasons 7 (2007–2013)
Born April 22, 1986, in Oakland, California

Marshawn Lynch is one of the most difficult players in the NFL to bring to the ground. Since being traded to the Seahawks in 2011, this powerful running back has been nothing short of incredible, rushing for more than 1,200 yards in three straight seasons. In his first career playoff game against the Saints in 2012, Lynch went into "beast mode," running for 67-yards and breaking nine tackles on his way to the end zone. Known for eating Skittles during games, this Super Bowl champion has a sweet tooth, but even sweeter moves on the field.

Richard Sherman

Richard Sherman was a fifth round **NFL Draft** pick by the Seahawks in 2011. Sherman is the most vocal player in the Seattle secondary, who are also known as the "Legion of Boom." The cornerback from Stanford University has recorded an incredible 20 interceptions in just three NFL seasons, and is widely recognized as the best cover corner in the league. He faced criticism for loud comments he made just seconds after tipping a pass intended for Michael Crabtree at the end of the NFC Championship Game in 2013. This athletic play helped the Seahawks punch their ticket to Super Bowl XLVIII.

Position Defensive Back
Seasons 3 (2011–2013)
Born March 30, 1988, in Compton, California

Earl Thomas

The Seahawks selected 20-year-old Earl Thomas with the 14th pick in the 2010 NFL Draft. The talented safety finished his rookie season with 60 tackles, a forced fumble, and five interceptions. His aggressive style of play leads to highlight-reel hits and terrified wide-receivers. The incredible speed in which Thomas is able to get to the ball allows him to play deeper than almost any NFL safety. Despite being so far away from the action, Thomas recorded 105 tackles in 2013, which was second on the team.

Position Free Safety
Seasons 4 (2010–2013)
Born May 7, 1989, in Orange, Texas

All-Time Records

9,429 — All-Time Rushing Yards

Running back Shaun Alexander played nine seasons for the Hawks and set nearly every team rushing record in the process.

97.5 — All-Time Sacks

In 13 seasons, all with the Seahawks, defensive end Jacob Green recorded close to 100 sacks. His greatest season was 1983, in which he tallied 16 quarterback sacks.

94 Single-Season Receptions

In 2007, Bobby Engram caught over 90 passes, breaking the record Darrell Jackson set in 2004 when he hauled in 87 receptions.

32
Single-Season Touchdown Passes

Although the all-time team leader is Matt Hasselbeck with 174 touchdown passes, Dave Krieg set the single season mark in 1984.

13,089 All-time Receiving Yards

Steve Largent is perhaps the most beloved Seahawk of all time. He had eight seasons with more than 1,000 yards receiving on his way to a 14-year, hall of fame career.

Timeline

Throughout the team's history, the Seattle Seahawks have had many memorable events that have become defining moments for the team and its fans.

1987
Steve Largent makes history, catching six passes to become the all-time leading receiver in NFL history (751 receptions). The Seahawks finish 9-6 in a strike-shortened season. They battle the Oilers in the wild card game before falling in overtime 23-20.

1976
Lloyd W. Nordstrom, who helped land an NFL team in the Pacific Northwest, passes away prior to the start of the Seahawks **inaugural** season. The Hawks would go on to finish 2-12 during their expansion season.

In 1997, the Seahawks are sold to Microsoft co-founder Paul Allen.

1970	1975	1980	1985	1990	1995

1978-1979
The Seahawks edge the Raiders on the road, becoming the only opponent to have beaten the Raiders twice in the same season in 13 years. The Hawks go on to finish 9-7, behind Steve Largent and his 1,168 receiving yards.

1983
In his first season as head coach, Chuck Knox helps lead the Seahawks to the AFC Championship Game, where they lose to the Raiders. Throughout the 1983 season, the Seahawks enjoy a distinct home field advantage. The roots of the 12th Man are taking shape.

1999
The Seahawks win their second division title in team history, under new head coach Mike Holmgren. Unfortunately, Dan Marino leads Miami on a game-winning touchdown drive to knock Seattle out, 20-17, in the first round of the playoffs.

2005

The Seahawks finish 13-3, earning home field advantage throughout the NFC playoffs. The Hawks cruise through the playoffs at home behind the 12th Man. In Super Bowl XL, they are defeated by the Pittsburgh Steelers, 21-10.

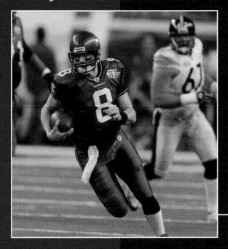

The Future

The Seahawks are loaded with talented players and are poised to be good for a long time. On offense, they boast a gifted quarterback in Russell Wilson, a tough running back in Marshawn Lynch, and exciting wide-receivers like Doug Baldwin and Percy Harvin. Defensively, Earl Thomas, Richard Sherman and Cam Chancellor are the "Legion of Boom," perhaps the most intimidating defensive group in the NFL. The Hawks are thinking **dynasty**.

In 2012, Russell Wilson, a third round pick out of Wisconsin, outplays highly paid free-agent quarterback Matt Flynn in the preseason and is named the starter.

2000		2003	2006	2009	2012	2015

In 2002, the Seahawks open their new stadium, and move back to the NFC West, where they played their inaugural season back in 1976.

2010

The Seahawks hire USC Coach Pete Carroll, who makes more than 200 roster moves in his first season. These moves and the following draft choices help engineer one of the greatest defenses in NFL history, and a Super Bowl victory in 2013.

2013

Behind Wilson, Lynch, a talented young defense, and helped by free agents Michael Bennett and Cliff Avril, the Seahawks finish 13-3, earning home field advantage. With the 12th Man behind them, the Seahawks play their rivals, the 49ers, with a trip to the Super Bowl on the line. Richard Sherman knocks down a pass intended for Michael Crabtree to seal a Seahawks victory. Two weeks later, against Peyton Manning and the Broncos, the Seahawks win their first Super Bowl Championship, 43-8.

Write a Biography

Life Story

A person's life story can be the subject of a book. This kind of book is called a biography. Biographies often describe the lives of people who have achieved great success. These people may be alive today, or they may have lived many years ago. Reading a biography can help you learn more about a great person.

Get the Facts

Use this book, and research in the library and on the Internet, to find out more about your favorite Seahawk. Learn as much about this player as you can. What position does he play? What are his statistics in important categories? Has he set any records? Also, be sure to write down key events in the person's life. What was his childhood like? What has he accomplished off the field? Is there anything else that makes this person special or unusual?

Use the Concept Web

A concept web is a useful research tool. Read the questions in the concept web on the following page. Answer the questions in your notebook. Your answers will help you write a biography.

Concept Web

Adulthood
- Where does this individual currently reside?
- Does he or she have a family?

Your Opinion
- What did you learn from the books you read in your research?
- Would you suggest these books to others?
- Was anything missing from these books?

Childhood
- Where and when was this person born?
- Describe his or her parents, siblings, and friends.
- Did this person grow up in unusual circumstances?

Accomplishments off the Field
- What is this person's life's work?
- Has he or she received awards or recognition for accomplishments?
- How have this person's accomplishments served others?

Write a Biography

Help and Obstacles
- Did this individual have a positive attitude?
- Did he or she receive help from others?
- Did this person have a mentor?
- Did this person face any hardships?
- If so, how were the hardships overcome?

Accomplishments on the Field
- What records does this person hold?
- What key games and plays have defined his or her career?
- What are his or her stats in categories important to his or her position?

Work and Preparation
- What was this person's education?
- What was his or her work experience?
- How does this person work; what is the process he or she uses?

Trivia Time

Take this quiz to test your knowledge of the Seattle Seahawks. The answers are printed upside-down under each question.

1 In what year did the Seahawks begin play as an expansion team?

A. 1976

2 Which NFL team joined the league the same time as the Seahawks?

A. The Tampa Bay Buccaneers

3 Who was head coach in 1983 when the Seahawks made it to the AFC Championship Game?

A. Chuck Knox

4 Which Seahawks wide receiver retired with almost every NFL receiving record?

A. Steve Largent

5 What is the name of the stadium the Seahawks play in?

A. Centurylink Field

6 How many touchdowns did Shaun Alexander run for in 2005?

A. 28

7 Who did the Seahawks play in Super Bowl XL?

A. The Pittsburgh Steelers

8 Russell Wilson is often compared to which hall of fame great?

A. Fran Tarkenton

9 What famous food does Marshawn Lynch eat during games?

A. Skittles

10 What team did the Seahawks defeat in Super Bowl XLVIII?

A. The Denver Broncos

Key Words

All-Pro: an NFL player judged to be the best in his position for a given season

dynasty: a team that wins a series of championships in a short period of time

expansion teams: brand new teams in a sports league, usually from a city that has not hosted a team in that league before

free agent: a player who is not currently under contract to play with a particular team

hall of fame: a group of persons judged to be outstanding in a particular sport

inaugural: marking the beginning of an institution, activity, or period of office

logo: a symbol that stands for a team or organization

merger: a combination of two things, especially companies, into one

most valuable player (MVP): the player judged to be most valuable to his team's success

NFL Draft: an annual event where the NFL chooses college football players to be new team members

passer rating: a rating given to quarterbacks that tries to measure how well they perform on the field

playoffs: the games played following the end of the regular season. Six teams are qualified: the four winners of the different conferences, and the two best teams that did not finish first in their respective conference, the wild cards

postseason: a sporting event that takes place after the end of the regular season

Pro Bowl: the annual all-star game for NFL players, pitting the best players in the National Football Conference against the best players in the American Football Conference

sacks: a sack occurs when the quarterback is tackled behind the line of scrimmage before he can throw a forward pass

Super Bowl: the NFL's annual championship game between the winning team from the NFC and the winning team from the AFC

Index

Log on to www.av2books.com

AV² by Weigl brings you media enhanced books that support active learning. Go to www.av2books.com, and enter the special code found on page 2 of this book. You will gain access to enriched and enhanced content that supplements and complements this book. Content includes video, audio, weblinks, quizzes, a slide show, and activities.

AV² Online Navigation

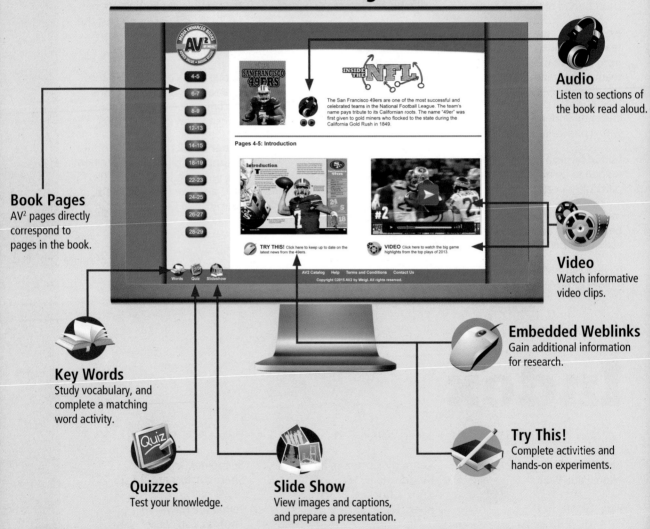

Audio
Listen to sections of the book read aloud.

Book Pages
AV² pages directly correspond to pages in the book.

Video
Watch informative video clips.

Embedded Weblinks
Gain additional information for research.

Key Words
Study vocabulary, and complete a matching word activity.

Try This!
Complete activities and hands-on experiments.

Quizzes
Test your knowledge.

Slide Show
View images and captions, and prepare a presentation.

AV² was built to bridge the gap between print and digital. We encourage you to tell us what you like and what you want to see in the future.

Sign up to be an AV² Ambassador at www.av2books.com/ambassador.

Due to the dynamic nature of the Internet, some of the URLs and activities provided as part of AV² by Weigl may have changed or ceased to exist. AV² by Weigl accepts no responsibility for any such changes. All media enhanced books are regularly monitored to update addresses and sites in a timely manner. Contact AV² by Weigl at 1-866-649-3445 or av2books@weigl.com with any questions, comments, or feedback.